To

From

Written and compiled by Sophie Piper
Illustrations copyright © 2013 Angelo Ruta
This edition copyright © 2013 Lion Hudson

The right of Angelo Ruta to be identified as
the illustrator of this work has been asserted
by him in accordance with the Copyright,
Designs and Patents Act 1988.

Published by Lion Children's Books
an imprint of
Lion Hudson plc
Wilkinson House,
Jordan Hill Road,
Oxford OX2 8DR, England
www.lionhudson.com/lionchildrens

ISBN 978 0 7459 6381 5

First edition 2013

Acknowledgments
All unattributed prayers are by Sophie Piper,
copyright © Lion Hudson.
The prayers by Lois Rock (pp. 15, 20) and
Mary Joslin (p. 28) are copyright © Lion
Hudson.

Bible extracts are taken or adapted from the
Good News Bible, published by The Bible
Societies/HarperCollins Publishers Ltd,
UK © American Bible Society 1966, 1971,
1976, 1992, used by permission.

The scripture quotation on page 40 is from
The New Revised Standard Version of the
Bible copyright © 1989 by the Division
of Christian Education of the National
Council of Churches in the USA. Used by
permission. All Rights Reserved.

The Lord's Prayer as it appears in *Common
Worship: Services and Prayers for the Church of
England* (Church House Publishing, 2000)
is copyright © The English Language
Liturgical Consultation and is reproduced
by permission of the publisher.

A catalogue record for this book is
available from the British Library

Printed and bound in China,
December 2012, LH17

Our Father

Praying with the words of Jesus

Sophie Piper

✤

Angelo Ruta

LI♥N
CHILDREN'S

Introduction

According to the Gospels, Jesus spent a lot of time praying. Sometimes he went off alone into the countryside to pray. Sometimes he stayed up all night. His disciples saw what he did and wanted to learn from him.

"Lord, teach us to pray," they asked.

"When you pray," Jesus explained, "go to your room, close the door, and pray to your Father, who is unseen. And your Father, who sees what you do in private, will reward you.

"When you pray, do not use a lot of meaningless words…. Your Father already knows what you need before you ask him. This then, is how you should pray."

He gave the very words his followers should use. This prayer is today known as the "Our Father" (from its opening words) or "The Lord's Prayer".

It is here presented line by line alongside prayers and reflections that shine a light on the meaning.

Our Father in heaven

Who may come into God's presence?

The person who obeys God in everything,
who always speaks the truth,
who keeps every promise,
who cannot be lured into doing wrong.

Such a person will be safe all through life.

From Psalm 15

Jesus said:
"I am the way, and the truth,
and the life. No one comes
to the Father except through me."

From John 14:6

O God,
as truly as you are our father,
so just as truly you are our mother.
We thank you, God our father,
for your strength and goodness.
We thank you, God our mother,
for the closeness of your caring.
O God, we thank you for the great love
you have for each one of us.

Julian of Norwich (1342–c. 1416)

Whoever loves is a child of God...
for God is love.

1 John 4:7–8

Hallowed be your name

O God, your greatness is seen in all the world!

I look at the sky, which you have made;
at the moon and the stars, which you set in their places,
and I wonder:

Who am I, that you think of me?

What is humankind, that you care for us?

O God, your greatness is seen in all the world!

From Psalm 8:1, 3–4

Our God is the God of all,
The God of heaven and earth,
Of the sea and the rivers;
The God of the sun and of the moon
    and of all the stars;
The God of the lofty mountains
    and of the lowly valleys,
He has His dwelling around heaven
    and earth, and sea, and all that in them is.

St Patrick (389–461)

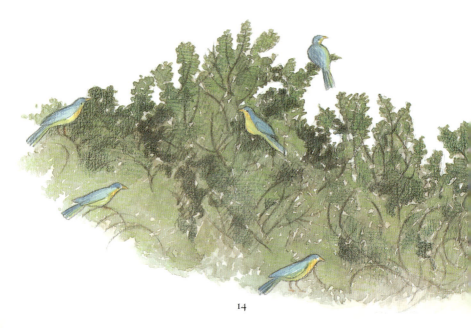

I think of the diverse majesty
Of all of the creatures on earth;
Some with the power to terrify
Others that only bring mirth.
I think of their shapes and their colours,
Their secret and curious ways,
And my heart seems to long for a language
To sing their Great Maker's praise.

Lois Rock

Your kingdom come

Jesus called the children to him and said, "Let the children come to me and do not stop them, because the Kingdom of God belongs to such as these."

Luke 18:16

May I seek God's kingdom
more than richest fare
trusting God will feed me
as the wild birds of the air.

May I seek God's kingdom
more than cloth of gold
trusting God will clothe me
as the wild flowers that unfold.

May I seek God's kingdom,
may I choose the way
of holiness and goodness
to Heaven's eternal day.

*A prayer based on Jesus' Sermon
on the Mount, Matthew 6:24–34 and 7:13*

The kingdom of God
is like a tree
growing through all eternity.

In its branches, birds may nest;
in its shade we all may rest.

A prayer inspired by Jesus' parable
of the mustard seed, Matthew 13:31–32

Your will be done
on earth as in heaven

Jesus said:
"Follow me.

"Anyone who starts to plough and then keeps looking back
is of no use to the Kingdom of God."

From Matthew 8:19–22 and Luke 9:57–62

Like the ox that ploughs so straight
with slow and steady plod
May I learn the humble ways
to live as pleases God.

Lois Rock

Day by day,
dear Lord, of thee
three things I pray:
to see thee more clearly,
love thee more dearly,
follow thee more nearly,
day by day.

Richard, bishop of Chichester (1197–1253)

Jesus said:
"Do for others what you want them to do for you."

Matthew 7:12

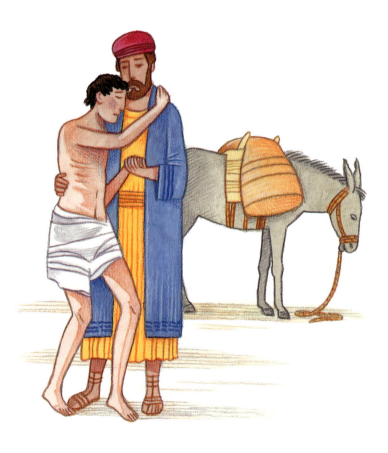

Lord Jesus,
Make me as kind to others
as I would want to be to you.

Make me as generous to others
as I would want to be to you.

May I take time to help them
as I would want to take time to help you.

May I take trouble to help them
as I would want to take trouble to help you.

May I look into the faces of those I meet
and see your face.

Based on Matthew 25:37–40

May I be no one's enemy, and may I be the friend of that which lasts for ever.

May I never quarrel with those nearest: and if I do, may I be quick to restore the friendship.

May I love only what is good: always seek it and work to achieve it.

May I wish for everyone to find happiness and not envy anyone their good fortune.

May I never gloat when someone who has wronged me suffers ill fortune.

When I have done or said something wrong, may I not wait to be told off, but instead be angry with myself until I have put things right.

May I win no victory that harms either me or those who compete against me.

May I help those who have quarrelled to be friends with each other again.

May I, as far as I can, give practical help to my friends and anyone who is in need.

May I never fail a friend who is in danger.

When I visit those who are grieving, may I find the right words to help heal their pain.

May I respect myself.

May I always control my emotions.

May I train myself to be gentle and not allow myself to become angry.

May I never whisper about wicked people and the things they have done, but rather seek to spend my time with good people and to follow their good example.

Eusebius (3rd century, adapted)

Give us today our
daily bread

Jesus said:
"I am the bread of life. Those who come to me will never be hungry; those who believe in me will never be thirsty.
"I will never turn away anyone who comes to me.
"For what my Father wants is that all who see the Son and believe in him should have eternal life."

John 6:35, 37, 40

Give us, O God, the needs the body feels,
Give us, God, the need-things of the soul;
Give us, O God, the balm which body heals,
Give us, God, the soul-balm which makes whole.

Poems of the Western Highlanders

May God clothe me,
may God feed me;
may God guide me,
may God lead me;
may God comfort
and defend me,
with encircling love
befriend me.

Mary Joslin

Lord, for tomorrow and its needs,
I do not pray;
But keep me, guide me, love me, Lord
Just for today.

Sister M Xavier (1856–1917)

Forgive us our sins

Jesus said:
"All who make themselves great will be humbled, and all who humble themselves will be made great."

Luke 18:14

I told God everything:
I told God about all the wrong things I had done.
I gave up trying to pretend.
I gave up trying to hide.
I knew that the one thing to do was to confess.

And God forgave me.

Based on Psalm 32:5

God, have mercy on me, a sinner!

From Luke 18:13

O God,
Lift me when I fall;
forgive me when I fail.

Every day is a new beginning
woken at dawn by the birds' glad refrain.
Though yesterday's troubles
and long ago sorrows
may trouble the soul
and awaken old pain,
a day is beginning,
the shadows are fading:
in heaven's new light,
joy will be born again.

As we forgive those who
sin against us

Jesus said:

"If you forgive others the wrongs they have done to you, your Father in heaven will also forgive you. But if you do not forgive others, then your Father will not forgive the wrongs you have done."

Matthew 6:14–15

Seven
times seven
I freely forgive
and seven
times seventy more.
Lord, give me the grace
to forgive
and forgive,
again
and again
I implore.

Based on Matthew 18:21–22

Lead us not into temptation

Jesus said:
"Keep watch and pray that you will not fall into temptation. The spirit is willing, but the flesh is weak."

Matthew 26:41

I will walk with Jesus.
– But you may be betrayed.
I will walk with Jesus.
– But you may be abandoned.
I will walk with Jesus.
– But you may be given a cross too heavy to bear.
I will walk with Jesus.
– But you cannot know where that may lead.
I will walk with Jesus.
– Then may Jesus walk with you through life and through
  death.

A prayer inspired by Matthew 16:24–27

But deliver us from evil

Jesus said:
"I am the resurrection and the life. Those who believe in me will live, even though they die."

John 11:25

I will not worry,
dear God,
but I will ask you for the things I need
and give thanks.

Give me the peace that comes from knowing that all
my worries are safe with you.

From Philippians 4:6–7

The Lord is my light and my salvation;
I will fear no one.
The Lord protects me from all danger;
I will never be afraid.

Psalm 27:1

The Beatitudes

Jesus not only gave his disciples a prayer. He also told them what would lead to true happiness.

"Blessed are the poor in spirit, for theirs is the kingdom
of heaven.
Blessed are those who mourn, for they will be comforted.
Blessed are the meek, for they will inherit the earth.
Blessed are those who hunger and thirst for righteousness,
for they will be filled.
Blessed are the merciful, for they will receive mercy.
Blessed are the pure in heart, for they will see God.
Blessed are the peacemakers, for they will be called children
of God.
Blessed are those who are persecuted for righteousness'
sake, for theirs is the kingdom of heaven."

Matthew 5:3–10

Ask, Seek, Knock

Jesus encouraged his followers to pray and told them this:

"Ask, and you will receive;
seek, and you will find;
knock, and the door will be opened to you.

"For everyone who asks will receive,
and anyone who seeks will find,
and the door will be opened to those who knock.

"Would any of you who are fathers give your son a stone when he asks for bread? Or would you give him a snake when he asks for a fish? Bad as you are, you know how to give good things to your children.

"How much more, then, will your Father in heaven give good things to those who ask him!"

Matthew 7:7–11

"How much more, then, will the Father in heaven give the Holy Spirit to those who ask him!"

Luke 11:13

From the Bible

The prayer that Jesus taught is said by Christians all over the world. There are versions in many different languages. Even within a single language there are often several versions that use slightly different words.

Each of them is based on the two versions of the prayer in the Bible.

One is from Matthew's Gospel:

Our Father in heaven:
May your holy name be honoured;
may your Kingdom come;
may your will be done on earth as it is in heaven.
Give us today the food we need.
Forgive us the wrongs we have done,
as we forgive the wrongs that others have done to us.
Do not bring us to hard testing,
but keep us safe from the Evil One.

Matthew 6:9–13

The other is from Luke's Gospel:

Father:
May your holy name be honoured;
may your Kingdom come.
Give us day by day the food we need.
Forgive us our sins,
for we forgive everyone who does us wrong.
And do not bring us to hard testing.

Luke 11:2–4

Our Father in heaven,
hallowed be your name,
your kingdom come,
your will be done,
on earth as in heaven.
Give us today our daily bread.
Forgive us our sins
as we forgive those who sin against us.
Lead us not into temptation
but deliver us from evil.

This ancient prayer is often said as an ending:

For the kingdom, the power,
and the glory are yours
now and for ever.
Amen.